D1610411

The Stone Sleep

by

Raine Geoghegan

First published 2022 by The Hedgehog Poetry Press

Published in the UK by
The Hedgehog Poetry Press
5, Coppack House
Churchill Avenue
Clevedon
BS21 6QW

www.hedgehogpress.co.uk

ISBN: 978-1-913499-53-2

9 8 7 6 5 4 3 2 1

A CIP Catalogue record for this book is available from the
British Library.

Front cover imagery © Dr Hannah Brockbank

I dedicate this work to my father James Charles Hill who left this world far too soon and my sister Beverley Maryan (nee Hill.)

'He tends his white flock on the green hillside
He helps each stone in the inherited red cave to give birth.'

   - 'St Sava the Shepherd' – *Vasko Popa*, Poet.

'Nature is what we know – Yet have no art to say –
So impotent Our Wisdom is to her simplicity.'

   - 'Nature is what We See – *Emily Dickinson*, Poet.

Contents

THE STONE SLEEP

"Even asleep we partake in the becoming of the world" – *Czeslaw Milosz, The Magic Mountain.'*

To escape her gaze,
you give yourself to the earth as it whispers
sleep, sleep.

Sinking into the mossy bed,
the grass bends beneath you.
Here in a foetal shape, back in the womb,
are you breathing?

Night folds itself around you,
a ghost moth settles onto your cold skin,
whispering a lullaby.

Others join her,
breathing and singing until wing to wing
they cover every part of you.

In your dreams you try to remember
who you were before you closed your eyes.

..... always moving
aware of the hard edges
wanting to be curved
bending, breaking
small breasts
a slightly rounded stomach
thin hands
skin smooth the colour of olives left in the sun
bare cracked feet
her deep eyes heavy with life shut tight .....

At dawn a shroud of powdered wings
rise up to leave you naked.
You see, yet don't see, feel, but don't feel,
still the earth whispers,
sleep, sleep.

As the light unwraps itself,
you go deeper into the stone sleep,
into the slumber of the drugged,
into the sleep of those who cannot sleep.

MASKS

one by one, our masks
are taken away and hung
in a closet

remember the first time
you looked in the mirror
how your eyes lit up
like two new planets
waiting to be discovered

I AM THAT SALMON

She dives deep
 into crisp green waters,
splices through changing currents,
springs up towards the sun
then down into
the pleasing watery arms..
Above her, a fish,
or something foreign
shimmying in the light.

A split second and she is there,
opening her mouth in anticipation,
closing it on a sharp sly hook
Spawn like bubbles pop around her.
Flashes of blue, green, yellow
fade into grey.
Pulled out of the river,
she is thrown onto an alien bed.
It is dry, coarse.
She lies choking, quivering,
ripples of water spill onto the bank,
never to reach her.
*'I am that salmon as the hook is taken out of her mouth and I watch the
light*
in her eyes slowly fade.'

WILLOW FEELS THE CHILL OF WINTER

Sharp frost fills the air.
The ground hardens.

Stripped of colour like the sky,
you shed your leaves and weep.

As you turn inwards
Merkstave crawls into your trunk
while the earth groans.

You are more stone than bark.

Once you gave refuge to wolves.
They leapt into your branches,
slept at your feet, listened for Odin's footsteps,

he who wandered through the woods,
bearded, one-eyed. When he lay down at night
the wolves licked his hands.

Is this what you long for?

Merkstave: German/Runic word for confusion

THE CLOSE OF THE DAY

At the close of the day,
she stops doing what she's always done.
Opening the door, she
tiptoes into the quiet house.

At the close of the day,
she sips nettle tea,
writes a shopping list,
calms the whining fridge.

At the close of the day,
she shuts her fears in a box,
walks between the rooms,
saying goodnight to the walls.

At the close of the day,
she learns to breathe again,
slow and deliberate. She strokes the cats and
listens to their tales, like she used to.

At the close of the day,
she stops, turns the mirror to face the wall,
slips out of her skin,
and dissolves into the cold bed of night.

'A SONG TO REST THE TIRED DEAD'

im of Celia Lane

it is dusk
she has come to wash the body
a table is set by the bed
a bowl of lavender water
clean muslin cloths
a white towel

  'too young for death'

she thinks as she removes all the clothing
and jewellery from the body of her niece
she notices stretch marks on the thighs
how the breasts have dropped
from feeding the chavies

  'forty years ago, just been borned
  sucking at her Daya's breast.'

taking a cloth
she dips it in water
squeezes it hard in her hand
sets about her task

malts stand by the door way
aunts, daughters, sisters and the daya
singing in low soft voices
a song to rest the dead

she speaks quietly
to her loved one as she gently cleans
lifting one arm up then the other
holding it
placing it down carefully
as if it was made of glass

the others won't move too close
it is mokkadi to do so

this woman who washes the dead
now holds both feet
letting them rest for a while
blessing them for all the miles
they have trod the earth

she dresses her niece in the finest of clothes
combs her dark tangled hair
places the gold chain and earrings in the palm
of the right hand
puts the wedding ring back on
the third finger of the left hand

   'such small fingers'

bending forward, kisses them

   'you are ready now my gel, sov well'

Chavies – children; Daya – mother; Malts – women; Mokkadi – unclean; Sov – sleep.

THE GLASS DELUSION

Don't touch me   I may shatter,
speak to me   walk around me,
but don't touch me   I may shatter.
I may break.
You can look at me   even look through me,
just don't get too close.
Shss, speak softly, quietly
don't raise your voice   I may shatter.
Sit close   but not too close.
I need plenty of space.
Don't judge me ...   if you do
I may shatter.
If the light shines   at just the right angle
you might see yourself reflected in my face.
Please don't scream   I may shatter,
if I do   you'll have to pick up the pieces.

(Inspired by Radio 4's programme 'The Glass Delusion')

THE HOSPICE ON A FRIDAY AFTERNOON

Breathing in, out.
Her eyelids quiver.
Yellow daffodils sit in a blue vase.
Next to it a cup of tea that has gone cold.
A sucking sound,
the syringe driver keeping my mother sedated and calm.
I brush her hair, teasing it a little so that it doesn't look so straight.
Her breath takes her further and further into eternity,
and as her face softens,
it becomes opalescent.
Her chest, rising, falling,
her limbs still, I remember her dancing at my wedding,
all smiles and dressed in peach.
Her skin glows in the afternoon light.
Her beauty deepens like the evening.
I draw close, breathing in the deep peace.
Safe with my mother,
mother safe with me.

LUDGATE SHOPPING CENTRE

She parks the car,
places blue badge on the dash.
The boys jump out,
slamming doors.

> *She feels the first prick of tension.*

Into the lift,
grey and smelling of disinfectant.
Status Quo singing 'Down, Down'.
Did she really like this band once?

> *Relief as they come to the first floor.*

Her son is happy, has a friend,
he's about to spend his birthday money.
The smile on her face is for him.

The boys rush into shops,
scan shelves; he wants computer games,
and new trainers,
a gentle reminder of how much cash he has.
A girl screams,
she jumps, nowhere feels safe.

> *She starts to fade, legs feeling like damp sand.*
> *'Stay upright'.*

They want to go into another store.
She promises them a pizza if they're quick.
She waits,
a cold wind stings her face.

> *Imagine a quiet room...somewhere in Ludgate*
> *shopping centre.*
> *A place to lie down,*
> *where limbs, bones rest inside skin.*

She considers going into the store.
Images of glass doors swinging,
bright lights, babies crying and musak,
forcing itself into ears, eyes, head.

> *A deep thirst and a*
> *yearning*
> *for soft earth, grass,*
> *the healing tones of green. She*
> *sighs as if breathing out will help*
> *her remain solid.*
> *Her legs give way.*

> *Crumpling to her knees,*
> *she slides down the shop window*
> *and in front of her, his feet.*

MY HANDS

I

I sit with my hands opened.
My right thumb protrudes from my wrist,
a visible sign of arthritis.
When fitted for my wedding band,
the shop assistant said, 'such *small fingers,*
a child's size.'
There are lines that have hardly changed,
unlike the ones on the back of my hand.
They have altered over time.
These unchanged lines, what do they reveal,
how long I will live,
will I be wealthy; the number of children I will have.'
I marvel at all the things my hands have done,
from clinging to my Mother's breast to self-pleasuring.

II
My hands seek expression.
In ballet they are gently held,
the thumb and forefinger almost touching.
My dance teacher would shout.
'*Soften your hands.*'
In jazz, they are fully stretched
or placed in fixed positions,
angular, bold.
In Indian Kathak they practise mudras.
'*The prana mudra being the gesture of life,*
the ring and little fingers are placed at the tip of the thumb,
the other two fingers are stretched upwards,
they move to the beat of the tala,
finally coming together in Pranam
to say 'thank you.'

III

My hands remember the soft folds
of skin at my Mother's throat as she nursed me,
how she gripped them as we crossed the road.
They went numb and couldn't breathe.
I washed my hands a lot when I was a child.
I liked the feel of cool water running over them
and the smell of Coal Tar soap when they were dry.
I sit with my hands opened
and see my Mother's hands, deft, swarthy,
always working, picking apples,
knitting jumpers, cooking pies,
polishing the brass, combing
the tangles from my damp hair,
then the stillness of them
as they lay on her chest at the hospice,
silently saying,
'my work is done.'

KAYAK SICKNESS

"When too much light falls on everything, a special terror results." Peter Freuchen." *

In your small boat
on a sheet of glass
you silently pray to Sedna.

Keep still, be patient,
then the seals will come close.

There is no wind. Light fills your eyes.

The soul empties itself,
feeding lake and sky.

Kayak hunters know this, right?

In this place,
you are floating.

You cry out but the sound is lost.
Your body, poised with a harpoon,

suddenly impotent.
breath quickens.
The heart beats loudly
disturbing the silence.

You see your family sitting at the empty table.

Waiting.

*Peter Freuchen's quote is taken from Pilgrim at Tinker Creek by Annie Dillard.
Sedna: Goddess of the Sea in Inuit Mythology*

FATIGUE

was something i relished, nestling in my bed
after a long day,
sleeping a healthy sleep,
that i would return
to the world.

now it is something monstrous
attacking my body,
furring my tongue,
clinging to my lungs,
embedding itself in my brain,
gnawing at my bones.

there are bars around my bed
and the door, like my mind, is shut tight.
I lie here day after day,
sleeping an unhealthy sleep,
tasting the bitterness of rust.

ME/CFS - Chronic Fatigue Syndrome

SHAMANKA

It is hot.
She places her bag of bones,
feathers and clumps of earth onto the dusty pavement,
sits in the heat of the afternoon sun.
She remembers that other country,
how she sat for three days and three nights with the bodies,
knowing that her presence helped their souls to migrate.

     'She rubs the bodies with red ochre soil,
curls them into a foetal position in the grave,
along with a few treasured possessions.
She covers them with herbs and wild flowers,
steps back chanting their names,
bidding them farewell.
She knows this ritual well.'

Three days, three nights,
that's how long it takes.
She picks up her bag.
Everything she needs is inside.
She travels lightly.
Hovering like a kestrel she waits to alight,
wherever she is summoned.

Shamanka – female Shaman, ancient healer.

DID YOU SAY GOODBYE

(im James Charles Hill)

On that day, was it pelting down with rain,
like it always did in Bedwelty?
Or was the September sun filtering into the room?
Perhaps the radio was on with Jim Reeves
singing one of mum's favourite songs.

Could you hear voices coming from the kitchen
as Nanna kept busy,
flip flapping the welsh cakes on the griddle ?
I imagine your gaze falling upon my small form,
my mother scooping me up, holding me tight.

Did you notice the creases of anguish in her face
as she let you have one more sip of whisky?
Did you give me one last kiss when she carried me away?
Did you know it was the last day?
Resting now,

on top of the hill,
overlooking the valley.

I've tried to find you,
but the grass has grown too high.

TATHAGATA – ONE WHO HAS GONE BEFORE

A daddy long-legs rests on the windowsill,
as if contemplating.
Buddhist monks
tread softly, mindfully.
They cast their eyes downwards
looking for the smallest of creatures;
Anything that moves,
is sentient.
Sometimes you will see them bending, brushing,
another creature saved from harm.
They are often smiling.
They know ...
life is an illusion.
What is real, is unreal.
What is unreal, is real.
They practise being still ...
when the mind is still
everything returns to balance.
Still the mind
and it becomes
the moon floating
like a silver boat
on a calm lake.
Still the mind
and it becomes a mirror
that has no blemish.

The daddy-long legs has fallen
into the sink.
Its fragile legs quiver as the water washes over it.

KALI MA

Goddess of Transformation
follows me home from Ireland
after an encounter on a Drama therapy course.
She sits in the middle of the wooden floor
with her many arms outstretched.
At times she is quiet,
sleeping with her three eyes open.
Red bangles and jewels fall around her waist;
silver bells adorn her dark ankles.
How long is she going to stay?
She isn't like other visitors.
She frightens my friends when she exercises her arms
and brandishes her sword.
It's getting worse;
she's started stamping her feet,
the earth is cracking open.
She's dancing wildly in the garden,
hurling abuse at the neighbours.
I've asked her to leave.
She laughs and sticks her long red tongue out.
She doesn't notice what is happening to me.
I stay in bed, stop eating,
sleep, dream of who I will become.
When I wake,
she is there, comforting me with her many arms.
She makes me laugh when she rolls her eyes
and waggles her long red tongue.

(Kali Ma – Hindu Goddess of death and rebirth, also known as the Goddess of Transformation) Written after attending the Heroes Journey in Kilkenny, Ireland, 1995

WILDFLOWERS

She is tying bunches of wildflowers, placing them into a penerka, her arthritic hands working slowly. She stops, breathes in the fine fragrance, remembers the flowers made of paper, she used a small peg knife to curl the petals, taking it up and over, one by one, taking time until they looked like the real thing. Then the small bunches of heather that she cut and put together in tissue paper with a thin piece of bass tied around the ends.

She is walking with the vardos, holding the hands of her youngest children. Her husband is guiding the grai, she is singing an old song, 'I love to walk along the drom, in the month of May, kushti divvus, kushti divvus, it's a kushti day.'

She is in her vardo, birthing her fourth child, the one with the strawberry mark on her back. Great Aunt Carrie is bathing her forehead. After screaming and cursing, the welcome cries of her daughter, reminding her of the first flush of a mother's love.

Sitting on her dada's knee, singing a song about lollipops, her voice breaking as he bounces her up and down, his laughter mingling with hers.

Now she lies on a hospital bed, her face chalk white, her eyes watering, her Granddaughter sitting close by on a hard backed chair, her fingers moving, like sea anemonies, pushing, pulling, pushing, reaching out to her Granddaughter who is transfixed. '*Picking the flowers, smelling the scent, tying them up, two bob a bunch, 'kushti divvus, in the month of May.'*

Penerka – basket; Vardos – wagons; Grai – horse; Drom – road; Kushti divvus – a lovely day.

27

THE LUNGO DROM

Bare,
blistered feet.

She walked
over stone
on grass
through thicket and brush
in water,
snow,
flowers and mud.

Her hair grew long,
flowing like a river.
Tiny silvery fish latching
onto each tendril,
longing for the open sea.

At night
she slept in bushes, caves, beside trees.
She dreamt of fire.

She drank from streams,
picked heather, lavender, rosemary for healing,
exchanged them for bread,
kept on walking.

Her hair turned white.
Her bones thinned.
Her body bent over
and her eyes grew weak .
Still she kept on moving.

One early morning under a mottled sky
she stopped.
The moon shone in her body.
Light fell on the ground
and she knew
this was her atchin tan.

Romani jib (words): The lungo drom - the long road; Atchin tan - stopping place/home

DARK EYES

when the moon is high
the air static
she hears the grey wolf
howling

she sits on the earth
her head bent over
her long hair falling into mud

the smell of her sex
mingling with that of the rich soil

once she gave birth
in a barren place
a washcloth a pitcher of water

or was it blood
so much blood
her baby silenced at birth

a grey wolf with dark eyes
licking her face
its tongue cool, abrasive

he sat with her
as she cried
long tears
his soft howling brought peace

for a long time
they were both still
then he led her back to her tribe

when he left, she cried

when the moon is high
the air static
she hears the grey wolf once more.

IN APPRECIATION

I wish to thank Mark Davidson at Hedgehog Poetry Press for his support and generosity and for publishing three of my pamphlets. Thanks also to James Simpson, my mentor and friend who has guided me along my literary path and has inspired me to do my very best. A special mention to my friend Brenda Baynes for all her support, to both Sarah James and Geraldine Clarkson for their wonderful endorsements, to Dr. Hannah Brockbank for creating the beautiful design for both front and back cover and last but not least my family, Simon, my tender, caring husband and my daughter and son Becky and Luke who are always there for me.

PRAISE FOR THE STONE SLEEP

"This extraordinary and exquisitely-crafted pamphlet, the third from Romani poet Raine Geoghegan, has a unique silver thread running through it, of winter, sleep, stone... A tree is 'more stone than bark', a woman is stone, and tries to escape feeling; fatigue makes stone of another person. Of course the ultimate sleep is death, and there are poems which feature a woman finding her final 'atchin tan', or stopping place, on the road; a vigil is kept with a loved one nearing the end of their journey; a young woman is prepared for burial according to Romani customs; and a gravestone is searched for, lost in long grass. Rituals of birth, death and sex are celebrated. And behind the 'stone sleep' of the title is a huge and indomitable life spirit. As the epigraph to the opening (and title) poem, taken from Czesław Miłosz, says: "Even asleep we partake in the becoming of the world". This life spirit, wild and resilient, is embodied in nature, animals (the wolf, the hawk), native cultures, and elemental presences. Kali Ma, the Hindu goddess of death, rebirth and transformation, presides over the work, representing feminine power, subversive and rebellious: 'she laughs and sticks her long red tongue out'. The Inuit goddess of the Sea, Sedna, also features, and a female shaman, 'like a kestrel'. The Salmon, symbol of rebirth, is hunted for cruel human sport, while another poem celebrates the Buddhist reverence for the smallest living creature. Like the 'masks' and 'eyes' and 'hands' which appear, this very tightly-themed pamphlet is greater than the sum of its parts. *The Stone Sleep* is nourishment and guide: it will be a delight for Raine Geoghegan's regular readers and is sure to attract many more to her compelling and healing work."

-GB Clarkson, Author of 'Overcoat of Flesh.'

"Sometimes shamanic, always moving, these are stirring slivers of living and loss. From 'As the light unwraps itself,/ you go deeper into the stone sleep' to reaching atchin tan (stopping place/ home), this pamphlet evokes and awakens a new sense of being and belonging."

-Sarah James, Poet and Editor at V. Press.

ACKNOWLEDGEMENTS FOR THE STONE SLEEP

Thanks are due to the editors of the following publications in which some of these poems have previously appeared. *Anima Poetry Press 2017: The Meeting House, a Poetry Anthology with the Chichester Stanza Group 2018.* 'The Stone Sleep'; *Anima Poetry Press 2017:* 'Masks'; *Indigo Dreams Press: For the Silent 2020.* 'I Am That Salmon'; *The Curlew Magazine 2019.* 'Willow Feels the Chill of Winter'; *Anima Poetry Press 2017 & Impspired Literary Journal, Volume 4 2020.* The Close of the Day; *Culture Matters 2020 & Poethead, online showcase 2020.* 'Song of the Tired Dead'; *Fly on the Wall Press: Please Hear What I'm Not Saying 2019.* The Glass Delusion'; *Poetry & Jazz Cafe Magazine 2017.* 'The Hospice on a Friday Afternoon'; *NHS Poetry Anthology: Body and Soul 2019, longlisted in NHS Poetry competition 2021.* 'Fatigue'; *Wagtail Press: Romany Women's Poetry Anthology 2021.* 'Shamanka'; *Chichester Stanza Anthology 2019.* 'Did You Say Goodbye?'; *Fair Acre Press: E-Book on Spiders 2018.* 'Tathagata'; *Impspired Journal Volume 4 2020.* 'Wildflowers'; *Writing in a Woman's Voice online Journal 2021.* 'Dark Eyes'; *Words for the Wild Nature Journal & Poethead, online showcase of women writers 2020.* The Lungo Drom.